For This I Live

Katherine Ross

innovo
PUBLISHING

Published by
Innovo Publishing, LLC
www.innovopublishing.com
1-888-546-2111

Providing Full-Service Publishing Services for
Christian Authors, Artists & Organizations: Hardbacks, Paperbacks,
eBooks, Audiobooks, Music & Film

FOR THIS I LIVE

Unless otherwise noted, all Scripture quotes are from the Holy Bible
King James Version.   Scripture quotes marked CW are from The Clear
Word Copyright © 1994 by Jack J. Blanco (fourth edition). Printed and
distributed by Review and Herald Publishing Association.

ISBN 13: 978-1-61314-230-1

Cover Design & Interior Layout: Innovo Publishing, LLC
Illustration: Rosa Cheryl Swint

Printed in the United States of America
U.S. Printing History
First Edition: July 2014

Dedication

This book is dedicated, first and foremost, to my Lord and Savior, Who knew me before I was formed in my mother's womb (Jeremiah 1:5) and Who has delivered me for such a time as this (Esther 4:14). Also, to my beloved mother, father, sisters, brothers, and my dear sons, Joseph Thurman Jr., Tavis Neville, and Kendrick Neville—God has blessed me to be a part of your lives.

This book is not intended to cast judgment on anyone's character or actions because only God can judge the heart. "Judge not, that ye be not judged" (Matthew 7:1). ". . . God the judge of all . . ." (Hebrews 12:23). It is solely written to shed light on my humble beginning and how a Higher Power has safely guided my life.

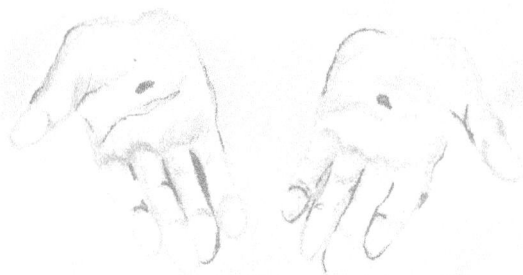

Preface

God brings one through struggles and challenges in life so he/she can go back and help someone else come through with as little difficulties as possible. He is in the business of saving lives with the Son, Holy Spirit, and whosoever will (Revelation 22:17)—young, old, rich, poor. I choose to be one of the whosoevers, by the grace of God, by writing this book to inspire all those who read it. No matter what trial you might face in life— seemingly unaccomplished goals, born into a family with no mother or father present, godly lifestyle not practiced in the home, others helping to raise you—God sees all, knows all, and, like He delivered Moses through the Red Sea, Daniel from the den of lions, and freed the demon-possessed man, He can do the same for you in your hour of darkness if you truly seek His guidance.

Each person's situation in life is an object lesson (the person involved is the object to his/her lesson) being taught. Meaning one should learn from his own experience. This book is a compilation of events in my life and how I was able to discern these teachings to bring me into a closer relationship with God. Being in partnership with God will truly help make life sweeter than ever. The love of God is emphasized throughout the pages of this book, showing how He wants to save us all in good times and bad.

I offer my blessings to those who supported me with encouraging words, prayer, or purchased my homemade cookies in support of my book. And to the wonderful staff at Innovo Publishing, especially Darya Crockett, Dr. Bart Dahmer, and Lindsay Olford.

Table of Contents

The Early Years

It seems like only yesterday I was running around and playing on that farm in the country with nothing to think about except eating, sleeping, and fun. Mom and Dad separated when I was two years old, so I grew up mostly in a single-parent home with my daddy and five siblings in the rural area of Cordova, Tennessee. They all called me "Sissy," but I didn't like it. I can't forget that white wood frame house with three rooms, a kitchen, and hardwood floors throughout. We had a potbellied wood-burning heater for heat, and for cooking we had a Superior brand black stove with a white porcelain oven door and two overhead ovens that were mostly used for keeping food warm. There was no bathroom. Baths were taken in a tin tub, and we had an outhouse for a toilet. The house was not wired for electricity, so we had no air conditioner. Back then, I really didn't know the difference. It was a way of life for Daddy, but God's fresh country air was just the best ever. There was a well beside the house and a thick row of hedges in front of the house. Two trees in the front produced plenty of shade for sitting out in the evenings. The maypops and honeysuckle plants gave off a sweet fragrance in the summer, and sometimes I would taste the nectar while exploring on the farm. I was very careful with picking the wild blackberries and strawberries that grew along the fence because snakes were known to hang out in the berry bushes.

Daddy was a sharecropper on a vegetable farm. He worked, planted, and harvested that land, sold crops at the market, and still had time to raise six children to the best of his ability. Being the youngest, I often got extra sweets from Daddy. Until I was old enough to know better, I thought my sister, Imogene, was my mother because she handled me with a mothering touch; she never scolded me. I remember her telling me one day, "You know now that I am not your momma, so stop calling me Momma."

I played silly games and was obedient until it was something I did not want to do, like washing dishes. I protested by sulking and moving slowly, but that was soon put to rest. I had a vivid imagination when it came to playmates. My brothers did not want to play with me all of the time, and my sisters were too old to play the games I played so, basically, I was alone most of the time (except for my guardian angel).

Cowboys and Indians was one of the games I played. My horse was a mop handle, and I considered the strings to be the horse's head. I used a stick or plastic gun as my pistol. My favorite place for riding was to the field where Daddy was working. He would either be plowing the ground with an old mule, preparing it for planting, or harvesting the vegetables. I can remember two mules on that farm that did all the plowing and cultivating of the land. I would mount my horse and gallop all the way to where Daddy was. I followed at a distance because I had been told to never get too close to the mules; they might become frightened, causing them to buck and kick. Sometimes I would stay there all day watching him until his workday ended or I decided to go on another farm adventure.

Before I went home, I would stop by some of the vegetable plots and have a raw meal of sweet potato, tomato, turnip, or whatever suited the cowgirl's appetite at the time. At home, I'd eat what was in my reach, which was usually a peanut butter sandwich, apple butter sandwich, buttermilk and cornbread, or molasses on cornbread until my sisters decided to cook. My older siblings complained constantly about the food Daddy provided—shelves of canned beans, dry beans, rice, flour, cornmeal, apple butter, peanut butter, etc. They said they were tired of it and refused to cook it, so sometimes Daddy would cook. He had always said we were poor, but I ignored it, until I was an adult and realized the truth. I didn't want to appear poor, so I never invited friends over because we had no electricity. There were only two of us families in the neighborhood without electricity.

I rejected the customary wearing of an outfit two straight days to school before washing it. I alternated my outfits to make sure I looked different every day. I washed my clothes every evening and took baths in the morning instead of at night, as we were told to do. At night, I would put two kerosene lamps together to cast a brighter light to appear to have electric lights. Now I can freely say the word *poor* because I am.

There was an old house on the right side of our house that Daddy used as storage to keep old furniture, dishes, and clothes. No one ever moved into the empty house on the left. My brothers called it the haunted house. I used the storage house as a playhouse; I cooked my mud cakes on the old stove. My brothers would hide there when they were in trouble. I would hide under the clothes.

As for the empty house, there was definitely something creepy about it. We were told to stay out of it. I supposed Daddy didn't want any windows broken. I wasn't too keen on hearing someone talking back to me, repeating exactly what I had just said, through a window. They told me it was called an echo. Nevertheless, I didn't like it.

Nothing has been as heaven-like to me as my childhood years. I had not a care in the world. I loved my daddy. He was a mild-mannered, peaceful abiding man. Nothing or no one could ever take his place. I loved my sisters and brothers, and I also loved that farm.

God was there at this young tender age, teaching me work ethics through Daddy; we learned by example. Daddy didn't have to say, "When you get older you will have to get a job." Each of us understood that. Paul wrote in 2 Thessalonians 3:10, "If any would not work, neither should he eat." The concept of living off another is wrong. Lying in wait to steal what another has worked hard for is wrong.

God has equipped all of us with an abundance of talents and gifts; we have to figure out what those gifts and talents are. He created all of us with a purpose in mind, not for selfish desires but to serve others more than ourselves. Life is an object lesson. Every situation we encounter in life has meaning, so disciplining the mind is crucial. Hidden deep, beyond my knowledge at that young age, He was molding me. He showed me how to mother my sons, being that one day I would have to embrace the role of a single parent, just as my dad did. God also showed me how to survive in life with just the simple things and how to give the best to others. Too many people are concerned with having big houses, fancy cars, and expensive dining. We need to learn to just live within our means (budget). We must not use unethical means to acquire worldly possessions or teach that it's all right to covet our neighbors' belongings (Exodus 20:17).

I can't forget Daddy and the mules. When he put the bridle and bits on those mules and connected it to the harness he wore in order to guide them, it didn't appear to be easy. Sometimes he would stumble when trying to get the mule back in place because it wanted to go its own way. He would put blinders on the mules so they couldn't see all the distractions. Daddy had to connect with those mules every day in order to discipline them. That reminds me of how God has constantly been in my life. Daily I come yielding my life to Him in order to stay focused on my Christian walk. He has not given me all the directions for my life journey all at once, lest I become confused. He tells me just as much as I can remember and perform daily. There are a lot of distractions in the world "that leadeth to destruction . . . because strait is the gate, and narrow is the way, which leadeth unto life" (Matthew 7:13–14). Years ago, I read this anonymous quote: "The highest evidence of nobility in a Christian is self-control."

Trying to Fit In

I must have been a little pest to my two older brothers because they always played games where they would hide from me, like hide-and-seek or sending me on errands to get something and then running off. I often cried when I could not find them. Sometimes I tried to hold on to their clothes to keep them from running away. They would hit me hard on my hand until I turned loose or they would just push me away. Soon I got tired of that so I became friends with our Italian neighbor's grandson, David, and our white neighbor's sons, Paul and David. Yeah, more boys, but they were my age. My Italian friend, David, would help his great-grandmother pick tomatoes and beans, water the plants in the hot bed, or just run around in the special area we had been given to play in. With Paul and David, we would throw balls back and forth, and sometimes maypops, across a wired fence that separated our houses. If the maypops hit and burst on you, that was cause for laughter. Even though we were friends, I was never to cross that fence. There was always a watchful eye on us at all times (their mother or my sisters). Back then, parents and older siblings always watched out for the younger kids, even while playing. It's just the way things were. I believe they all had as much fun playing with me as I had with them. I don't know if they were taught to be prejudice, but I was not.

Another fun place on the farm was a shallow creek, about one-fourth of a mile from the back of our house. I often watched my brother's fish in it. They did not take the time to teach me how to fish so I tried to catch fish in a pan. Sometimes they would leave the house as if they were going fishing and take me with them. When we got to the creek, they left one by one until I was left alone there; they told me they were going swimming. When I got tired of fishing, I would walk over to where Daddy was and rest. Sometimes, he would give me a ride home on his tractor.

God knew that one day I would have to interact with people of different ethnicities, and I was to treat them all the same. I was not to practice partiality toward them because God Himself is no respecter of persons. He accepts all nationalities (Acts 10:34-35; James 2:9). If we would accept the fact that in the household of God we are all family, then perhaps racial barriers, slurs, and prejudice would cease. When I reflect on that time in my childhood, it was the beginning of the Civil Rights Movement. As children, we were already bringing about unity, and we had no knowledge that we were doing so. They were my first friends. The neighborhood was a mixture of blacks, Italians, and whites, and they were all friends of Daddy.

It is not a sin to admire the beauty of Gods' created beings so long as the lust of the flesh does not overrule good judgment.

I try not to burden myself with unnecessary worldly cares, so I try to laugh as much as possible. It is good to laugh. God created laughter. Abraham and Sarah laughed (Genesis17:17, 18:12) when God revealed His plan for them to have a child in their old age. Solomon said there is "a time to every purpose under the heaven . . . a time to laugh" (Ecclesiastes 3:1, 4). But like everything else, laughter should be done in moderation.

The Neighborhood Store

Our neighborhood store was located on Highway 64, a two-lane highway about one-fourth mile from our house on the same side of the road. That was one of the good things about going to the store alone; I never had to cross the highway, but my brothers did. I only crossed the highway when I was with my brothers. They said it was safer to walk facing traffic. The store was owned by Italians but not related to our neighbors. I remember the first time I was asked to run an errand to the store. My sister Josie wrote a note, signed it, and folded it up with money inside. She instructed me to give the note to Mr. Johnny or Mr. Caesar. In those days, if the store owner didn't have what you wanted, they wrote it on the note. Josie stood at the end of the driveway and watched me as I walked along the gravel shoulder of the highway. I stopped and stood in the ditch when the big trucks passed by because I was scared of them. The wind from the trucks would almost blow me down.

When I walked into the store Mr. Johnny asked me, "Where is your note?" I handed it to him. I liked both Mr. Johnny and Mr. Caesar, but Mr. Johnny was the nicest. He always gave me a peppermint stick. Daddy said it was all right to accept it as long as I did not ask for it. My sisters and brothers said that Mr. Caesar was cheap (he never gave out peppermint sticks). Mr. Johnny put everything in a bag with the change and gave it to me along with my peppermint stick. He walked me outside to watch me off to a safe start back home. I didn't have any fear of anyone bothering me. I was only scared of the big trucks.

There were times when I had to take the mail to the mailbox and pick up the incoming mail. Either my parents had a lot of trust in me at five years old or they were too lazy to do it themselves. I didn't mind because it seemed like I was in charge. I felt responsible and accountable, qualities for which I was sure to need in the coming years.

In those days, asking for anything was considered begging, and that was never acceptable. I believe God was instilling in me the importance of having a strong work ethics. Laziness is not of God. However, it is not a sin to save or be frugal. Mr. Caesar was a wise man.

God gave me assurance that I would never have to walk alone. My sister and storekeeper were indeed watching out for my safety, but He was there too. The idea of being safe was once a minimal concern in my community. Most gunfire was from killing rabbits, squirrels, deer, etc. (of which I detested). I would sleep outside for hours into the night on the warm hood of Daddy's car without any mishaps. Today, violence is rampant in every neighborhood; there seems to be no restraint or control. It is beyond man's control to stop it. Only God can, and will, end it for good. In the meantime, thanks to the many Christian outreach reform centers. God regards life as something precious and valuable. If not, then why would He be concerned about Abel (when Cain killed him), or why would He send His only Son (a Godhead) to die for me (a mere creation of His hands from dust) so I can have eternal life? Taking time to be educated in the ways of God will stop the fear of not being safe.

Facing Those Early Growing Pains

I was around five years old when I started noticing the strange way I reacted to people. Whenever Josie and Imogene's (my sisters) friends, or our cousins, came to visit, I would hide in another room. I did not want to talk. I was always told to stay out of grown-ups' conversations and to play in my room. I was told I shouldn't be sitting around grown-ups. Although my sisters were just teenagers, they considered themselves grown. I had to stay out of their business, so I locked myself in another room. While in the room, I would eavesdrop on their conversations. I think they knew because I could hear them talking about me sometimes. Josie would say, "Sissy is too grown." Her friend and my cousin would say, "I believe she is shy, Josie." That was true, but Josie would say, "That girl ain't shy; she's too grown and has her way too much." At the time, I didn't know exactly what Josie meant. "Daddy don't treat her like he treated us at her age; she gets away with things we couldn't." That was puzzling to me. They didn't realize my inner struggle.

I was extremely shy as a child, and hiding was the only way I knew how to deal with it. I began to dislike it when anyone came to the house because I got tired of hiding out. Sometimes when I was on punishment and couldn't go outside to play, I would open the windows for fresh air. Besides eavesdropping, I played games that I made up in the window so I could enjoy the cool air coming through. When I got older, I would read, clean up, or do homework until company left. The shyness was so bad that I would refuse to talk when I was away from home. I stood either holding my Daddy's leg or I just stood behind Josie or Imogene. If anyone asked me, "What's your name?" one of my sisters would say, "You can talk. Tell them your name." When I didn't respond, the person would say, "Oh! Cat got your tongue?" All I wanted was to be left alone. I had no idea that so many labels could be attached to someone for being shy. Through the years, I got called square, stuck up, and antisocial, but thanks to the Lord, it did not hinder me from going forward.

Not wanting to talk much was a natural-born gift from God. I don't have to worry about staying out of people's business. Paul (2 Thessalonians 3:11; 1 Timothy 5:13) talks about tattlers, gossipers, and busybodies wandering from house to house idle speaking things they ought not. In Romans 12:18, Paul wrote, "If it be possible, as much as lieth in you, live peaceably with all men." I was wrong to eavesdrop on my sisters but, on the positive side, perhaps it helped me become a good listener. Now, I enjoy listening to, and helping solve, other people's problems.

Instead of exuding negativity, a voice should be used to uplift the name of Jesus, drawing people to Him. I am still a shy person, but when I have to present Jesus His blood covers me. I realize that He is my life support. Every breath, every heartbeat, every flicker of the eye, every piece of bread I eat, every word, and every sentence I speak comes from God.

Church

Daddy attended an old family Baptist church in Mt. Pisgah—a community in rural Cordova, Tennessee—until he later changed to Seventh-day Adventist. He took all of us to church with him. Daddy read the Bible every night before going to sleep. I can't remember him ever missing a night reading by that old oil lamp with his glasses perched on his nose. He read to the younger ones too. Later, the older ones started going to the neighborhood church by themselves. My older brother Eddie and I still had to go with Daddy. Sometimes my sister took me with her to go to church with the older kids. I never really understood the moaning bench ritual.[1] My sister, her friend, and our cousin were on the moaning bench at the same time. I heard them talking about it taking a year for one person to come off the bench. I'm so glad I never had to do that.

I loved singing those old hymns like, "Swing Lo, sweet chariot, coming for to carry me home," or "I come

---

[1] In old Baptist churches, when a young person, usually around twelve, felt he/she was ready to join the church during revival meetings, they would sit on the front pew to avoid distractions from their peers. While sitting there (moaning bench), they were prayed over, preached over, and songs were sung until they felt the Spirit and jumped up shouting. This was evidence he/she was ready for baptism.

to the garden alone while the dew is still on the roses," or "On a hill far away stood an old rugged cross . . ." Those songs brought warmth, comfort, hope, and peace to the struggle I had deep within. Daddy sang in a quartet, and I loved to hear him sing.

I have heard many say that you don't have to go to a building to worship God; that is true. The *real* purpose behind going to church is for strength and to be fed spiritually. After six days of toiling on this earth, it does the mind and soul good to see others striving to accomplish the same goal—a closer walk with our Maker. With like-minded believers, you can talk about your daily walk, encourage each other, and fellowship with one another (Hebrews 10:25). The Word of God is how we gain knowledge of Him and talk to Him through prayer.

When trouble came later in my life, singing those old hymns was soothing to my soul; I even tried to sing in choirs. It wasn't until years later, while taking voice lessons, that I realized I was not a singer, but I did as the psalmist instructed: "Make a joyful noise unto God . . . Sing forth the honour of his name: make his praise glorious" (Psalm 66:1–2). I still make a joyful noise, and I still love those soul-searching songs.

Auntie

Daddy had a sister we simply called Auntie. She did not have any children. She was so helpful and always willing to help Dad with us, especially me, like combing and plaiting (braiding) my hair when my sisters weren't home. She was so sweet; we all loved her.

Since Auntie could not drive, Uncle Arthur would drive her to our house and drop her off. Daddy would take Auntie home after he got off work. I loved to ride with them. Auntie, Uncle Arthur, and Daddy often took us for walks along the train tracks at the back of Auntie's house. It was fun and a bit scary. If we heard the train blow from a distance, they got off the tracks and walked alongside the tracks. I always ran away because it was very frightening to me. When the train got closer, Uncle Arthur showed them how to motion to the conductor to blow the whistle. That was fun, but only at a distance.

My sisters and brothers often went to work in the cotton fields across the highway from us. They said it paid more money than on the farm. They would babysit Eddie and me in the field. They made Eddie a little cloth sack to hang over his shoulder to put cotton in. I played beside them until they got tired of me, and each took turns carrying me on his or her cotton sack.[2] That was so much fun. However, my wandering days were rapidly coming to an end. Oh what peace was mine; oh what a joy divine.[3] I soon had to leave all this safety and security behind.

There was excitement and uncertainty in my heart because I was about to change course in my young

---

[2] This was a long sack that hung from the shoulders to the ground and, unless you were very tall, the end of the sack was flat on the ground. This was what I rode on and slept on.

[3] Inspired from the song "Leaning on the Everlasting Arms" by Elisha A. Hoffman, 1887, public domain.

life. I was going from the known (playing on the farm, attention, fun) to the unknown (school). I had heard talk about school and it sounded good, but how would I fit in? Would I be safe and secure? Would I like school? Would I miss being at home? I would soon find out when I started school.

Oak Grove

Cling! Cling! Cling! Cling! Cling! Cling! I could hear that old hand-rung school bell ringing more than a quarter of a mile away. It was my very first day at Oak Grove Elementary School. I was so excited and tried to take everything in at once. I had seen this school many times, driving by with my daddy and going to church with my siblings. The church was about one hundred yards away from the school, but I had never seen the inside of the school. The school and church were both painted light blue. The school was a four-room building that looked like a house that sat just off the highway. The rooms were large. The first room had one female teacher who taught first and second graders; she was also the principal. There were two adjoining rooms on the left. One had a female teacher who taught third, fourth, and fifth graders. The other room had a female teacher who taught sixth, seventh, and eighth graders. The fourth room, the kitchen, was located in the back of the first room, which was my classroom. It had a large coal-burning heater for heat, a small area was where we put our coats and hats, and a window that was kept open for air. We would take turns putting coal in that old heater, but I didn't like all the black soot I got on my hands.

Seeing familiar faces in a different setting seemed odd to me. I was as excited as any first-time pupil could be. We walked to school except for a few who lived a mile or more away; their parents drove them to school or they rode with other students. There was no busing for the elementary school at that time, but that soon changed. Bussing was only for the high schools.

When I got to school, I could hardly wait to get on those old squeaky swings. But the bell would always call us to class. Our school day started with devotion, which included a song, a prayer, and the pledge of allegiance. Later, we had Bible verses to recite. My favorite was the Golden Rule: Do unto others as you would have them do unto you. Of course, I learned later that what we recited was not exactly as it is stated in the Bible. The actual quote says, "Therefore all things whatsoever ye would that men should do to you, do ye even so to them . . ." (Matthew 7:12).

I don't recall the order of lessons we had for the day, but I loved the three R's: reading, (w)riting and (a) rithmetic. My favorite story of all was *Dick and Jane*. I imagined I was Jane. I used to think, *One day I will write my story*. I found basic arithmetic simple, but later on algebra was another story.

At lunchtime, I'd hurriedly eat my lunch and head for the swings. One day, I was awaiting my turn to swing when suddenly someone picked me up. I cried, "Put me down!" It was one of the older students in the seventh grade—daughter of the sixth-, seventh-, and eighth-grade teacher. She said, "Calm down, now. You were about to get hit by the swing. You were standing in the swing's danger zone." She did not allow anyone else to swing until I got my ride. She even gently pushed me until my turn was up. She was like a guardian angel from that day forward. Unfortunately, when her eighth grade year was up, she went to another school. During that time, there was no law that said you had to attend school after the eighth grade, so a few stopped going.

I loved going to school; it opened up a new world to me. Something about learning always inspired me. I was fascinated about learning to write, and I knew that one day I wanted to write my story. I became more involved in reading books and making new friends. Those were the most vulnerable years of my life. I realized just how much I had been sheltered.

I made up my mind that I was going to complete school and never miss a day. At that particular time I didn't pray it; I just knew it was going to happen. No one in my family had ever finished school, and I was determined to succeed.

Shadowlawn

Not only was it my first year of school, but it was my brother Eddie's first year as well. I asked him later in life why Daddy did not send him to school at age six. He said he had to work, and that hurt my heart. The two years we spent in the same classroom at Oak Grove Elementary was a lot of fun. Oak Grove eventually closed and at the beginning of our third-grade year, we were bused to Shadowlawn Elementary. Daddy had been instructed on the time and place we were to catch the bus. The bus driver would arrive at 6:15 a.m. He was so nice. He always waited until everyone was seated before driving off. It was so exciting to ride on a school bus for the first time, almost like starting the first grade.

When we finally got to school, I fell in love with it. It was much larger than Oak Grove, and it had a huge playground. A teacher met us at the bus and took us to the cafeteria/auditorium. We were instructed to sit and wait on the bell to ring (an electric one) and that our teacher would come get us and take us to our classroom. We had already been assigned a teacher. There were three or four teachers for each grade from first to eighth. All the teachers from Oak Grove were transferred to the new school.

Everything was brand-new, and it took a while for me to learn my way around this big school. The school had a principal's office, a lunch room where you could buy breakfast and hot lunches, a ball field, and other areas for activities for the older students. There were many new students in class the first day at Shadowlawn, so the teacher had us introduce ourselves by telling our name, school we transferred from, bus driver's name, and any brothers or sisters attending there. Sadly, they put my brother Eddie in a different classroom. I felt so lost when they took him away.

They Took Him Away

It happened in school,
a place I thought was cool.
The teacher came in the class,
and said, "This can't last."
I felt so lost when they took him away,
I didn't know how I could make it in
school another day.
He was gone, gone, gone out of sight,
but he was just down the hallway.
I'd forgotten I'll see him again tonight.[4]

I was still attached to family members for security. It wasn't easy letting go, especially since I had no friends in school at the time. So I just followed Eddie around. The teachers noticed this and decided it was best to separate us so I would not be so dependent on him for everything.

---

[4] Katherine Ross, "They Took Him Away," original poem, 2013.

When Trouble Comes to You

During this time, Daddy had met a Seventh-day Adventist married couple from Eads, Lucille and Otis Bobo, and we all were taking a Bible study class. She and her husband worked as a team to keep the congregation together, especially those who did not have transportation. They would pick them up and take them to their home. The pastor would come in from the city to have service twice a month until an actual church was built in the area. Daddy was not one to travel to the city much, so we had much of our service and Bible studies at the Bobo's home. Mrs. Bobo made Bible class interesting for us kids because she would tell us baby Jesus stories. I had learned to read and could read the Bible some. It was so much fun going to their home on the Sabbath. There were other families there with their children as well as the Bobo's granddaughter. After service, Mrs. Bobo would serve us dinner. While studying with them, Daddy had stopped eating pork, not that he ate that much anyway. The only pork I ever saw him eat was neck bones. We had chicken for dinner every Sunday, but that was even before Daddy met the Bobos. My dad went with them to the big church in the city, and to me it seemed unfriendly, probably due to my shyness. It was so big that it felt cold all the time. We watched my dad get baptized.

I believe my dad really trusted the Bobos. Mrs. Bobo would often tell me, "You need your mother." I thought she was being nosey. Dad would take us to visit with Mom, so what more did I need? I was happy with things just the way they were. I enjoyed going to school, learning, writing, and reading my Bible.

I can't ever remember being as happy as I was at Christmas in 1957. I was seven. Daddy had bought me a doll named Judy. Judy was a pretty little doll with a green skirt made out of felt, a white blouse, and painted-on socks and shoes. Her hair was in a ponytail. After getting Judy, I didn't spend a lot of time playing with my old playmates or my made-up toys.

During my third-grade year, as I was trying to adjust from the separation from my brother in school, Daddy got his divorce papers and he took us to Mother's house so she could sign them. On the way, he said, "Sissy, you need to be with your momma. She needs to talk to you. She needs to tell you about things I can't." I was puzzled. I had already heard about menstruation, so what else was there? I don't know what my parents discussed that day, but before I could say "shoo fly," Eddie and I were taken out of Shadowlawn School and enrolled in Bartlett Elementary near my mom's house. I was not ready to move in with my mom and go to another school. I didn't really know her that well. My brother Eddie took a liking to everything.

Mother lived about a half mile from the road. Once back there, you could not see the road. When you turned onto the gravel lane a short distance, there was a house on the right with dogs barking all the time. Even though they were tied, I still had to get accustomed to that. It was okay as long as I was with my brother. After passing that house, there was a gate that had to be opened and closed behind you each time. If you didn't close the gate, the cows would get out. After that gate was a large barn and four pens that housed pigs. There was a block of salt in front for the cows to lick. The dusty path between gates was an eighth of a mile, and that was before we reached Mother's house. There were cows everywhere roaming and grazing that pasture. I was afraid of those cows and didn't feel I could walk around freely. I had nightmares of cows running after me. I felt secluded from the world. Mother had a large vegetable garden as well as peanuts. One day she asked me, "What can you eat? Can you eat a hamburger?" I said, "No ma'am, I can't eat ham. That's pork." I laughed about that with Mother later in life. She didn't have a car so we walked everywhere, but she provided for us and never left us alone.

Mother always took me fishing with her, but she had to bait my hook because I was afraid to touch the worms. But boy did it make me smile when I caught a fish! Mother's fiancé gave me a puppy, which was nice because I really didn't have anyone else to play with. My brother Eddie was always gone somewhere with his friends or hunting or rustling up cows with Mother's fiancé.

At Bartlett Elementary, each teacher had two grades. Initially, we had to walk about a mile one way until it was approved for the bus driver to travel that road to pick us up. The teachers tested my brother and saw that he was more advanced than the students in his grade, so they advanced him two grades. Now he was in his right grade. Once again, he was moved from me, but it was for the good.

My Brother and I

My brother and I,
didn't always, see eye to eye.
He'd say it was this way, I'd say another,
but that was my brother.
My brother started to work at age six;
I started to work at nine.
Six was too young, I said,
but nine was still kinda sad.
We started school together;
I could not ask for anything better.
He did not like this, being that Daddy held him back,
but God sent a teacher to put him on the right track.
He did good for as long as he could,
but the support he didn't have as he should.[5]

This period of my life was like a rollercoaster. I finished the third grade and started fourth grade at Bartlett Elementary. This was when the cat was let out of the bag. Mother told me that Daddy was not my real father. I just stared at her; I couldn't say a word. She even told me my real father's name, how much I looked like

---

[5] Katherine Ross, "My Brother and I," original poem, 2013.

him, and that my grandpa had left me some money. I asked, "Where is it?" She said, "You'll get it in due time." I could hardly believe this. *Why me?* I thought. *Why am I the only one who's not Daddy's?* To me, he was still my daddy and nothing would ever change that. This was sad news to me, but I didn't dwell on it. Instead, I built up a wall of defense, saying that from that day on I didn't want to ever hear it again. Daddy never told me that I was not his child and never did he treat me any different from my brothers and sisters. As far as I was concerned, I *was* his child. He was a very good man, and I never knew why Mother left him. I figured he could not have been too awful because he raised a child that was not his, and he knew it. This took me back to a scripture I had read: "A bastard shall not enter into the congregation of the Lord . . ." (Deuteronomy 23:2). I thought I was doomed! Everybody knew I was a bastard child, and I just knew I wouldn't be able to go to heaven. Oh! I wanted so much for God to love me and to accept me. I felt unaccepted, and it made me cry. I was too ashamed to ask for the meaning of this verse. I don't remember exactly when I overcame this fear, but God was there safeguarding my mind. I was protected by His shield as He shaped my thoughts. God drove out those old thoughts and filled my mind with something else.

If I had the ability to zap out certain parts of my life, it would be this part. I was confused a lot of the time, I felt different, and there was so much change going on it was almost too much. I felt that Daddy and I had been betrayed. Even though he knew I wasn't his child, it felt like we were in this thing together. I had to ask God to forgive me for thinking this way so it would not interfere with my love for my mother.

Out of School

I was about two months into the fourth grade when something happened—I'm not sure what—at Mother's house that caused Eddie and me to be placed back in Daddy's care. That made me happy. I never disliked my mother; I loved her, but I loved Daddy more.

One day, Imogene looked out the window and saw Eddie walking down the highway with a stick on his shoulder and a ball of clothing tied to it. That evening, Daddy investigated and found out Eddie had gone back to Mother's house. I was out of school most of my fourth grade year because my dad could not afford to send us to school; so we didn't enroll. I was so hurt; I didn't know what to do. I went back to my old made-up toys, but with a different twist. I still had my doll, Judy. Instead of using the mop for a horse, it became a wig to mimic Shirley Temple's hair. I had watched my brothers tie a string on a stick, prop it under an upside-down half-bushel basket, and use that to catch birds. They would put pieces of bread under their makeshift bird catcher to lure the birds to the trap. Now that I was not in school and didn't have much to do, I tried it. When I tried to raise the basket to get the bird out, it would fly away. Mother had given me a little washboard for me to wash my clothes on so I didn't have to use the larger one. So there I was washing anything that appeared to be dirty. I was so ashamed of not being in school that I didn't want my old playmates to see me.

I found out at an early age that my wants were bigger than Daddy's money, so it wasn't hard for me to ask if I could work on the farm. Daddy always said, "You need to marry you a rich man, Katherine." I would just laugh. He didn't realize that the era of a man taking care of his wife while she stayed at home was rapidly ceasing. A woman had to provide for herself if she wanted anything decent and have peace with it. I don't think there were any child labor laws during this time, and if so, they were not being enforced. I was paid fifty cents per bushel of beans and up to, but never over, fifteen dollars a week during the time I was not attending school. I remember the first dress I bought with my earned money—a hot pink wrap with tie sides and neck choke. My shoes were black patent. (When I eventually returned to school, I wore this dress and made sure no dust got on it.)

Although I lost a lot of time being out of school, I was beginning to experience the feeling of independence at nine years old. This opened the door wide for my future self-sufficient living. I was working!

The Bus Bully

Early one morning, the principal came to talk to Daddy out in the field where he was working. They talked a long time. My sisters and I watched from the window. When Daddy came to the house, he told us that the principal said he came to talk to him instead of sending the truancy officer. He was trying to save him the trouble of having to go to court because Eddie and I were not in school. By law, we were required to attend school at our ages. I was excited about going back to school, but at the same time, I didn't want to go back without Eddie because of what the mean kids would say. Daddy took me to school the next day, but it was too far into the school year for me to pass. Eddie was still with Mother. Being a grade behind haunted me for a long time.

After going back to school, I tried to keep my mind on my schoolwork so as not to get yet another year behind. Unfortunately, I wore invisible print on my back every day for all to read. It said: "You can do whatever you want to me." This is just one of the many things I endured while going to school.

The bus stop was at an intersection. The fenced property belonged to one of our white neighbors that Daddy bought buttermilk from every week. They also owned the cotton field where my brothers and sisters worked. He told Daddy we could pick up any fruits (apples, pears) or pecans that fall on the outside of their fence, but never to come inside. Eddie took him up on his offer. He gathered the fruits and pecans that fell outside the fence and sold them. I just gathered the pecans because the apples and pears always looked wormy. This was a great little business for me, too, until I started back to school alone.

I fell one morning while running to the bus stop and injured my knee. One of the boys on the bus wanted some pecans, but didn't want to pay me for them. I refused to give them to him. This made him angry, so he told the principal that I was stealing pecans and selling them. When I arrived at school, I got a bandage from my teacher to put on my knee. I was in the restroom tending to my knee when I was called to the principal's office. He had me sit down in a chair, and then he whipped me across my legs, mostly hitting that knee I had just injured. This caused my knee to bleed even more. I limped for over a week before it healed. I told my brother, but I never told Daddy. The boy who told on me thought it was funny. He was an eighth grader picking on a fifth grader. It's like the expression: there's nothing new under the sun, same games just different names. (I can empathize with bullied children.) I was glad this was his last year on the bus. I continued to pick up pecans, but eventually I stopped selling them.

During the next school period, I noticed that my friend began acting strangely toward me. It was as if I had become a stranger to her. In the cafeteria, she didn't sit with me. After school while waiting on the bus, I attempted to sit next to her but she moved. I couldn't figure out what was wrong. I was so confused. The next day we were outside for exercise and recess. We all went to get water, and she walked away with her new friend, with their arms around each other's shoulder. I followed. She turned to me and said, "Katherine, stop following me. You are not my friend anymore." I stopped in my tracks; I didn't know what to do. I felt like burying my head in the ground. What did I do? She turned toward me again and said, "Katherine, you are a square." They skipped away, laughing. I went back to the fountain to drink more water. I drank and drank, as if the water was going to wash away the hurt from what had just happened. While standing at the fountain, this boy who had a crush on me showed up. He tried to talk to me, but I ran away. I was not interested in him or any other boy in the sixth grade. After the incident with my friend, I didn't try to make any new friends, but if I was approached, I showed myself to be friendly. Isn't that what Proverbs 18:24 says? "A man that hath friends must shew himself friendly."

God knows already who I am, what I am capable of doing, and how much I can bear. So I have to tap into the tools He has already given me to accomplish His goal in my life. I must **love** my enemies and do good to those who despise me. I must have **patience** with those who I think do not measure up to my expectations. I must **humble** myself to this form of patience and accept the fact that I cannot do anything on my own; even my faith in Him comes from Him. I will **hate sin** and not the person who sins. Did I create a heaven and earth? Did I create male and female? Do I have all power and knowledge? So then how can I esteem myself higher than the next person? Love and forgiveness is my focus.

Uncle Henry

Okay, I've lost my friend. I've started this new life. Mother moved away, and Eddie is now back at home with us. We were all together again. That was swell, but I had no idea it was not for long.

My mother had a brother named Henry who was in the army. He would visit us every two years or so. He and his wife always had a gift or some money for all of us. We had no idea that Mother had asked him to come get me until she returned. What? Was I in some type of danger? Why this sudden change? I had no idea what or why this was transpiring. I felt safe and comfortable with Daddy. I was so tired of moving from house to house.

When Uncle Henry and Aunt Lena arrived to pick me up, the first thing he said to me was "Has your mother told you who your father is?" *Oh my goodness!* I thought. "Yeah, she told me," I answered slowly. Remember, I didn't want to hear that again for as long as I lived. So that was why he was there. Daddy had nothing to say in the matter, and he looked very sad. None of my sisters or brothers wanted me to leave. Everyone cried. I thought I would never see them again.

We left one Friday afternoon and headed for Lakeland, Florida. We spent the night in Vicksburg, Mississippi, with an army family Uncle Henry knew. It was so different being away from everyone at home. It was a new feeling I had never felt before. All the attention was on me. Uncle's friend had a daughter. Since it was not too dark to be outside, and there were plenty of streetlights, she wanted to skate. I fell because I had never skated before. Aunt Lena suggested putting a small pillow on my hind side. It looked so funny. Can you imagine a thirteen-year-old who had never worn a pair of skates? After skating, we ate, bathed, and went to bed since Uncle Henry said he wanted to get an early start home in the morning.

The next morning we had breakfast, the family fixed up some lunch for us to take with us, and we were on our way. Uncle Henry and Aunt Lena took turns driving. I never will forget that long highway across the Gulf of Mexico. Looking at all that water was scary, so I lay down. They kept saying, "Look, Kathy, that is the Gulf of Mexico." I raised my head and peeped. Water was as far as I could see. No land in sight. I tried to be brave, so I sat up in my seat with my eyes closed. I would open one eye slightly to see. It seemed like the highway would never end. I slept most of the way to Lakeland.

When we finally got to Lakeland, Uncle and Auntie's daughter, Vera, and her husband, Fenton, were there to greet us. Vera and Fenton had a daughter name Jackie. It was as though I was her little sister instead of a cousin. Vera took me to my room and helped me put up my clothes. She asked a lot of questions, but she was so nice. After getting settled in my room, Vera took me to eat and shop. She did that quite often. When we returned, I showed Aunt and Uncle what Vera had bought for me. Later that evening, after we all settled down, they told me the house rules:

> **Rule 1:** I am to do my chores around the house.
>
> **Rule 2:** I am to make only As and Bs on my report card. Uncle said, "C is for average people, and I expect you to be better than average." I respected this rule because this was what I always wanted. I tried even harder when I moved in with Uncle and Aunt but soon had to realize

that I could not make all As all the time. After studying hard, and all through the night, I would still make Bs and Cs on my tests. Thank the Lord that He gave me the ability to learn. I never gave up trying to make all As.

Rule 3: Uncle explained to me that I did not have to go to his church, if I did not want to go. He was pastor of the Church of Christ. He knew where the local Seventh-day Adventist Church was, and he would arrange for me to get there. I went to the Adventist church several times, but I felt out of place. I began to go to church with Uncle, but I never joined.

Rule 4: I will get fifteen dollars allowance every two weeks. Aunt told me I would have to buy all my personal hygiene items out of my allowance. I thought, *Wow, that much for an allowance!* This made me feel very important. That night, I slept in my own room, in my own bed, with my own television. For the first time, I didn't hear the far-off sounds of wolves howling. I closed my door and tossed myself from side to side in my bed, grinning the whole time. I didn't miss anyone! I wrote a letter to my daddy, sisters, and brothers every other day.

I noticed that all the houses in Vicksburg were built in the same style as those in Lakeland; they were low to the ground. Uncle had a two-car carport like most homes in the area. The laundry room was a room attached to the carport. It was a corner house painted a light blue in front and the other part was red brick. It had a master bedroom with a bath, guest bedroom, my bedroom, bath, uncle's office (where he spent most of his time), hallway, living room, dining area, and kitchen. The front lawn was neatly cut and trimmed with a palm tree on the side, and the backyard had three grapefruit trees (a fruit I love). I could eat as many as I wanted. I ate myself sick of grapefruit. For the first time, I saw palm trees, grapefruit trees, orange trees, and banana trees with bananas, which Aunt had grown. People picked oranges in Lakeland, Florida, like folks picked cotton in Cordova, Tennessee; it was a job. There was a bus that picked up workers the same as in Cordova.

Uncle and Vera showed me the way to walk to school. The street on the side of the house came to a dead end at a small orange grove with a path that had been marked by many years of kids walking to and from school. Those oranges were so sweet! A student later told me that they were there for the poor. The school, Lincoln Junior High, was about three-fourths of a mile past the orange grove.

New Kid on the Block

I don't remember what I wore that first day Uncle took me to school, but all eyes were on me. I was the new kid on the block. I was the most popular kid that entire year, even with my deep Southern accent. Even though Florida was farther south than Tennessee, the speech was quite different. Two classmates, Carolyn and Carol, befriended me on the first day of school. Carol's mother was our seventh-grade homeroom teacher, music teacher, and English teacher. While in school, Carol had to call her mother Mrs. Harris, the same as the other students.

My new friends briefed me on my schoolwork and walked me around the school. After a couple of days, they started walking with me part of the way home. Carol's mother had to stay after school for a little while, so Carol got permission from her. Carol was more on the talkative side and very nosey; whereas, Carolyn and I were more reserved, but we all seemed to blend in together. Carol asked me one day if I got an allowance. I told her, "Yes, fifteen dollars every two weeks." She said, "Fifteen dollars! Your uncle must be rich! My mother doesn't even want to give me three dollars a week." We all laughed.

It wasn't long after enrollment before the PE teacher/coach saw me run. Carolyn and I were racing and playing outside in the field. He told me I had great poise and running speed. He asked if I wanted to join the track team. I let him know I had to ask my uncle. I was shocked he said yes because I had gotten a C in music. I already knew I could run fast. We did have a track field of such back home, but we only used it to play racing games and softball. I wasn't good at hitting a ball very far, but running was my thing. Sometimes other players would ask me to run for them when they hit their ball if they weren't a fast runner. I would ask others to hit for me while I ran. I never let anyone run for me.

During the track meet competitions, there was always some girl there with legs longer than mine. I figured if someone had longer legs than me, they could run faster and I hated to lose. Nevertheless, I ran for the moon so if I should lose, I'd land amongst the stars. That's what I wanted to be—a great runner in the Olympics. I had a great support system. I got second place for running, third place for hurdles, and fourth place for the pole jump. I felt so important. Along with running, Uncle advised me to try out for swimming also. I didn't know how to swim so that meant I needed to take swimming lessons.

I picked a red one-piece swimsuit and enrolled at the Y, where two members from Uncle's church worked. There was always someone in the water to catch me when I pushed off from the wall of the pool with my feet. Someone had to hold me up while I pretended to float, do the backstroke, and so on. But there was no one to help me when I was supposed to hold on to the rail, duck my head and torso underwater, relax, and float back up. I did not float back up as soon as I thought I would, and I inhaled. I started fighting, but I eventually came up. I was instructed to do it again. I did and the same thing happened. This time, I felt like I was drowning. I took in too much water that time. They took me out of the pool, and I never took swimming lessons again. I would play in two or three feet of water but nothing more. Maybe one day I will try it again.

An incident occurred that made me think there should have been a fifth house rule, although one was never spoken. It was during a midweek Bible study at my uncle's church. I asked if I could miss the Bible study that day, and Uncle said okay. I had finished my chores and was sitting in the living room reading when the doorbell rang. I went to the door and no one was there. Just as I was sitting down, I heard a thump on the door, as if an object had hit it. I peeked out the window and saw no one. The doorbell rang again. As I opened the door, there was a boy standing there. Just at the same time, Uncle was pulling up in the driveway. That is all that happened. I was so nervous and afraid, even though I was innocent of any wrongdoing. I didn't know what Uncle was going to do. Uncle got out of the car and asked what was going on. I told him what had just happened. That was all I knew. He asked the boy what was going on. He said, his brother, Clyde, wanted to meet the family and was too shy to knock on the door, so he asked him (Freddie) to do it, but he didn't know we were not home. Uncle told him to go get his brother.

Clyde and Uncle talked. In short, Clyde was interested in me and wanted to become acquainted. He assured Uncle that he and Freddie had not been inside the house. Uncle introduced him to the family. Uncle sort of knew Clyde's father; they lived three houses from us on the next corner. Uncle said, "Kathy is not dating yet. You may visit sometimes, but you will be chaperoned at all times." I was so embarrassed. When Uncle pulled up and saw the boy there, I could see anger in his face. I didn't want him to lose trust in me. About two weeks prior to this incident, Carol told me Clyde had a crush on me. He had started hanging around us, and she said it was because he had an interest in me. I didn't believe her at first. "I know you are the reason," she said to me. "As long as I have known Clyde, he has never hung around me like that." She started calling me Mrs. Clyde Cherry. I would always smile when she did. I could tell he was cherishing those moments walking beside us. Carol thought Clyde was so savvy. He was so sure of himself. My aunt Lena and cousin Vera both agreed that he was very mature for his age. He was fifteen and I was thirteen. They loved having conversations with him when he visited. He wasn't hard to look at either. He had a nice smile and a gold tooth that was a replacement for a tooth he lost playing football. He liked to play chess, and so did Uncle. They tried to teach me a few times, but I couldn't catch on. I knew how to play checkers though.

Uncle's chaperone pick was an eighteen-year-old kid from his church, whom he trusted very much. His name was Donald. Whether Clyde and I were riding or walking to an event of any sort, there was old faithful Donald. He talked with us sometimes. Clyde was always on his best behavior at all times, even when Donald was not around. All he ever did was hold my hand. We had fun laughing one day about a remark Clyde had made. He said, "Donald has a crush on you too." I thought that was hilarious. The fifth house rule probably should have been, "Don't answer the doorbell when home alone."

Around the same time as that doorbell incident with Clyde, another boy from my uncle's church showed an interest in me; his name was Donnie. He was thirteen and in the eighth grade. He was a grade above me because I lost my fourth-grade year. He came to me at school and put a present in my hand. I told him I could not accept the gift. He insisted that I take it for friendship's sake. When I got home, I showed it to Aunt and Vera. They asked, "What is it?" I said, "A gift from Donnie. I told him I could not accept it, but he insisted." Vera told me to open it and see what it was. It was a key necklace. It read, "She who holds the key, can unlock my heart." Vera said, "That's too deep; it insinuates that you are dating. Why would he buy you something like that? He hasn't known you but, what, four months? I'm sorry Kathy, darling, but you must give it back." She asked me if I wanted to keep it, and I told her no.

Donnie came to visit Aunt and Uncle the next day after school. That was not unusual. He always visited them before I even moved there. We all noticed that he was wearing a heart pendant with a key pattern cut out of it. I was able to politely put the necklace into his hands without anyone looking and tell him I could not accept his gift. He said okay. Aunt shook her head and said, "Girl, you are too popular." I hoped that was a good thing because back at home I was not popular, or else I just didn't notice. Living with Uncle Henry and Aunt Lena was the highlight of my young life.

This was my first memorable trip outside of Tennessee. It was the first time I saw houses built different from those in Tennessee. The first time riding over a large body of water (compared to the Mississippi River). The first time two boys were interested in me at the same time. The first time I liked one. I was so blessed to have an uncle and aunt to treat me as if I were their very own child. God was making sure I didn't get completely lost in the growing pains.

I understand the phrase: it takes a village to raise a child. God already knew I needed to learn certain things that I simply was not going to get from being raised by a single parent. Uncle didn't sugar coat anything. He openly told me what most boys wanted from girls, and he did not want me sitting at home having a bunch of snotty-nosed, barefoot kids. He wanted me to stay focused in my books and have a great career. That was exactly what I had in mind also.

I had learned early before the trip to Lakeland that I had been gifted with being truthful. So it disturbed me terribly when I thought Uncle would lose trust in me because of a crazy incident that was completely innocent. Many kids I was not even friends with had "sworn me in" using the Bible to keep secrets for them. That was a great honor to me then, and now. I value trust, so I trust in the Lord.

God had given me just what I needed at the time. God didn't promise me sugar and spice, and everything nice, but He promised me eternal life at the end of this earthly life. God didn't promise me a stationary place to live on this earth, but He did promise, and has gone to prepare for me, a gated home in heaven. It has a wall great and high . . . twelve gates . . . and names written thereon, which are the names of the twelve tribes of the children of Israel (my ancestors). I don't have to worry about being a bastard child with no stable place to live because I am a child of God, and I have been washed and made clean by the blood of Jesus and His righteousness. For it is in Him I live, and move, and have my being (John 14:2; Acts 17:28; Romans 6:23; Revelation 21:12–21).

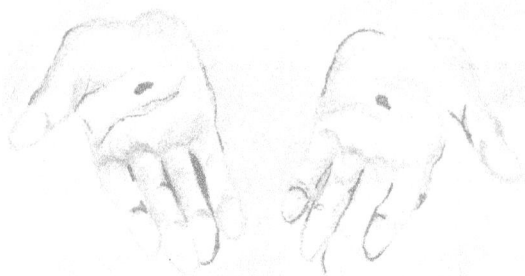

Living in a Fantasy World

I had made it to the eighth grade, and I felt comfortable with my new family. I was much more settled than I had ever been. Clyde was still coming to visit. My friends were still my friends, and track was at its beginning stage. Uncle and Aunt had asked Mother if she would allow them to adopt me, which was just fine by me. I don't know why, but Mother sent a letter to Uncle to bring me home immediately. Apparently, she didn't like the idea of letting them adopt me. So Uncle started making preparations to send me back as soon as possible, as per Mother's instructions. I asked him not to send me back, but he told me he had to do what Mother had asked. I cried so hard under my pillow that night, harder than I had cried when I left home to live with Uncle and Aunt. I tried to see the sense in going back, but I couldn't. I thought about going back in time of the old ways of Daddy and Mother. I was going back to those primitive ways of carrying water in buckets, heating water on the stove to take a bath, washing clothes in a tin tub on a washboard, having no electricity, sometimes cutting wood for fire when my brothers weren't around, making a fire in a wood-burning heater to keep warm, and old dusty roads. I didn't want to do that anymore.

Uncle contemplated putting me on a plane alone because he did not want to tackle that long drive, but he ended up accompanying me on the Greyhound Bus. When I was picked up at the bus station, he went back to Lakeland. I greeted everyone. I was happy to see them all, but I was not happy to be back. Mother was staying with Daddy until she could find a house of her own. Of course, she talked about how her brother (Uncle) tried to take me away from her. It seemed like every day she said the same old things. I never made a comment on the matter. However, I did enjoy being with her this time around. It gave me a chance to get to know her better. She had livened up things in that old house with no electricity. She had battery-operated radios, a small TV, and more furniture. It was different, but I still longed to be in Lakeland.

Mother decided not to work on the farm. She said, "I didn't like it back then, and I surely don't like it now." She found a job as a maid. I did babysitting for my two sisters when possible. I went back to the old Shadowlawn Elementary School. Riding the bus was a totally different experience than before. The older kids who would bully the younger ones were in high school now and no longer rode our bus. This made us the older kids now, but we did not pester the younger ones like the other kids had done to us. I tried to get excited about school and mingle with the other kids, but it was hard. I didn't neglect going to school or getting my schoolwork done because I loved school and learning. I had developed this love for good singing over the years, so I joined the school choir. I loved going to other schools and performing in plays.

Mother was always a devoted newspaper reader. Even now, she had the paper delivered to her; it was the *Memphis Press Scimitar*. There were certain parts of the paper she would keep. I started reading the paper as well. Through reading the paper and listening to the radio, I kept up with the outside world, and I was able to replace some of the void of missing my friends in Lakeland. My brother Eddie was dating, and Mother had told me under no circumstances was I to receive company until I reach the age of fifteen. That was okay with me. She said, "I heard about my brother having that boy come to his house. I don't know what's wrong with him, and then trying to take you away from me . . ." Still, no one could understand my feelings when it came to boys, and neither did I until I went to Lakeland. There was no one in the community I was interested in. I just wanted to go to school and get my education. I had big plans for my life.

With my babysitting money, and money I got from Mother, I bought a hand-held radio. After listening to the George Black Show, I joined his fan club. I got a free t-shirt and I could get discounts on other teen items. I enrolled four people in the club. That was not enough to make the club a success. The newsletter that was sent out every week had information from around the world. There was a section with names of people wanting a pen pal. I wrote to a girl named Jane in Australia. That might have lasted about a year; it took so long for the letters to get there. Jane wrote in one of her letters that she wanted to come to America to visit me on the farm. *She must be from a rich family*, I thought. I did not agree with it. My sister Josie always said I was living in a fantasy world. A fantasy world, perhaps, but it was my world, and I refused to allow my mind to be content with my immediate surroundings.

Another struggle had manifested in my life that was never shared with family members because I knew that God would see me through. I wrestled with it for two years but soon had to let it go. I thought maybe it was due to my constant moving from place to place, but I never was diagnosed so I don't know what it was. Beginning in seventh grade, I noticed a change in reading comprehension. It was slower than usual, and I watched how the other students were able to grasp quickly and move on. I had to reread several times, and I developed an inferior complex because of this. I studied by writing down important sections and memorizing it, but I was more determined than ever to succeed no matter what. I eventually just learned to live with it. Like always, I felt that extra push from the Spirit of God.

I understand from a parental point of view why Mother wanted me to come back home. Being a parent myself, I would never want my child to be raised by someone else as long as I am alive. I will look to God to give me full understanding when I get to heaven.

The Greenhorn

The ninth grade finally arrived, and I was already looking forward to my high-school graduation. For some people, the ninth grade was a wonderful grade to be in; it meant you had overcome eight years of intense learning.

But to the tenth and eleventh graders, you were just a greenhorn, and that's the look we freshmen got when we walked into Barrett's Chapel High School our first day.

Barrett's Chapel was farther back in the rural area than Shadowlawn Elementary. I remember Daddy saying, "Make sure you don't miss your bus because I will not be driving that far to take you to school." It was twenty plus miles one way. I only remember Daddy taking me a couple times, for safety's sake. Barrett's Chapel had a junior-high school attached to it and an elementary school down the road. It looked more sophisticated than Shadowlawn because it was supposed to have had more sophisticated students attending. It had more advanced labs, home economics, band, basketball teams, cheerleaders, and classes that were not at our former school. I tried to make the cheerleading team but was not chosen. I think my legs were not big enough, and I had no rhythm. The girls had to have a special PE uniform. It consisted of a blue snap-up jumper, white tennis shoes, and white socks.

I landed a job working in the school's office and so did another freshman named Olivia. It was a great honor for a freshman to be selected for this job. Many of the older students did not like the fact that I had been chosen by the principal. We had a slight advantage over the other students when it came to school events, such as games, free lunch, and a small stipend.

Our first basketball game was home game, and I still wonder if it was a dream that Daddy took me. I didn't hang out with him though, but I'm sure he didn't mind. I saw him talking to some of the other parents. It was one of the best times of my life. He didn't let me go to every game. Later in that year, Mother allowed me to ride the bus to the games. She was still living with us at the time. Eddie took me to a few games, and he tried to hook me up with his girlfriend's brother. This was the same boy who tried to talk to me at the drinking fountain a few years ago. He was bused to another school when we entered ninth grade. My brother had a four-door car, so I always sat as close to the door as possible, so as to not give Thurman any ideas. The others would tease him saying, "Man, you can't cross the barriers. You can't come to our school and try to steal our women." I was flattered and thought this was humorous and cute. They were all buddies because they were neighbors and, of course, I told everyone I didn't like him.

Thurman started driving his mother's car to our house after this. He always had a carload of his friends with him. He would ask for my brother first but ended up talking with my mother and sister. This went on for a while, and soon all of them were carrying buckets of water, cutting wood, and running errands to the store. Mother said, "If I work them, they will stop coming." At first, they all enjoyed Mother's and my sister Josie's good cooking. But sure enough, the carload soon dropped to one passenger. I thought that was funny. Thurman didn't come as often, but he did not stop coming. I think he felt like a part of the family by now.

I was blessed to make friends with several girls from other neighborhoods. Ninth grade was an adjustment period, but it left me trying to narrow down exactly what I wanted my career to be: writer, doctor, teacher.

Almost Defeated

In the tenth grade, I was already humming the "Pomp and Circumstance" graduation marching song. I thought, *I have made it. Just two more years.* I had narrowed my career choices down to elementary school teacher. I felt it would be much easier to teach and mold a student while he/she was younger because of the eagerness to learn. Becoming a doctor was eliminated because I couldn't stomach the sight of blood. Writing was still at the top of my list because I could better express my thoughts in writing versus talking; I had just pushed it to the side for a more convenient time.

Tenth grade brought on disturbing situations in and around school. It had been rumored that a boy was hiding beneath the stairs and grabbing the girls as they came down the stairs. The news was terrifying to most of the girl students. Unaware, and with my thoughts on getting back to class, I was attacked one day. I screamed. This boy grabbed my hands and pulled me to him so as to kiss me and muffle my sounds. I struggled hard, twisting around to get free. Suddenly, I remembered my sister Josie had told me how hard I could kick (I had kicked her a few times). I gave him two big kicks and when he turned me loose, I ran back to the restroom for help. The girls said they did not hear me scream. He was gone when the girls and I returned to the scene. The boy ended up attacking someone else and was later expelled from school. We never heard from him again. But for quite some time, I still felt the need to wash my mouth thoroughly from his kiss. I was angry. So angry that I lashed out in science class (the teacher had excused himself from the room) at one of the three male students I overheard talking about girls and dating. "Is this what you guys are all about? Why are you all always trying to take from us and abuse and violate us?" I asked angrily. One boy responded, "You're asking the wrong fellow; I'm not that way." I wanted to hear more of what the others had to say, but the teacher walked into the classroom.

***

It's not easy talking about assault, especially if you are the victim. Another disturbing situation was one where someone close to my family attempted to seduce me. I told Mother about it, and she handled it, but it left me angry. The incident that broke the camel's back happened about four years later at the age of twenty. I was married at the time. He was an associate of my husband. One day, after my husband left the house, someone rang the doorbell. It was his associate. He said he was looking for my husband. I said, "He just left. He just pulled off, did you see him?" That's when I saw the gun and heard the threats. It wasn't hard to figure out by the threats he made that he knew my husband's routine and had been spying on us. I don't know what this viciousness was called at the time, but today it is called aggravated rape. Something died inside me that day. And even today, that feeling tries to rear its ugly head, but I know God's sustaining power will keep me. All I have to do is call out his name and calmness overshadows me.

These incidents caused me to distrust in all males, at first. I trusted my daddy more than anyone in the world, and to be abused by another male was a huge letdown to me. I was constantly looking over my shoulder to see who was following me. I was uneasy being around men, even those at church. I feared opening my door. I had many nightmares of being assaulted, until one day in my heart I forgave them all—because they know not what they do (Luke 23:34). If they *really* knew God, they wouldn't commit such acts. I realized that this is a wicked world, and I have to fight for my right to be with God. He gave me the mind to forgive, forget, and go forward, forgetting those things behind and reaching forth for those things that are before me. I press toward the mark for the prize of the high calling of God in Christ Jesus (Philippians 3:13–14).

So many girls and women of today are victims of vicious crimes and many never report it. Some are too frightened, some don't want the media attention, and some don't want to be looked upon or made to feel like she was at fault (that was a common stigma in earlier times). Whether or not such a crime is reported, God says, "'Vengeance is mine; I will repay,' saith the Lord" (Romans 12:19). God will not put more on you than you can bear. This is derived from 1 Corinthians 10:13. This is the statement a sixteenth-century Bible commentator, Matthew Henry, wrote on the text: "Though it is displeasing to God for us to presume, it is not pleasing to him for us to despair. Either our trials will be proportioned to our strength, or strength will be supplied in proportion to our temptations. Others have the like temptations; what they bear up under, and break through, we may also. Men may be false, and the world may be false; but God is faithful, and our strength and security are in him. He is wise as well as faithful. He knows what we can bear. He will take care that we be not overcome, if we rely upon him. He *will make a way to escape*. There is no valley so dark but he can find a way through it."[6]

***

Since I was sixteen and getting close to graduation, I felt it was time to step out a little more on my own. To "step out" in those days meant you had to have transportation, and there were only three people I knew who had wheels: Eddie, Thurman (his mother's car), and Jean (my friend's brother's car). My mother did not approve of Thurman or Jean. She thought they were a bad influence on me. I learned that parents are God's gift to children. They have traveled the same road we try to go down. They should be given credit for knowing a lot more than their kids, but it's hard for kids, especially teens, to do.

Our high-school history teacher opened a malt shop for teens. I didn't think it was a place for me since I could not dance, but it was neat anyway. There was maybe one or two who would show up that couldn't dance, but not that often. Whenever I went with Eddie,

[6] Matthew Henry, *Matthew Henry's Commentary in One Volume: New One Volume Edition* (Grand Rapids, MI: Zondervan Publishing House, 1961).

he always had Thurman in the car. With Jean, it was just the girls. It was risky, but fun, because Jean did not have her license at first, so she drove the back roads.

Finally, Thurman asked me to go to the community picnic with him, and I accepted. Jean asked if we were dating and I said, "No, I just came to the picnic with him." She asked me, "Why not give him a chance?" Later on, we went to the fair and the malt shop together. So Thurman and I started dating. He tried teaching me how to drive, we went on double dates, to the movies, and we would take rides to the city. Thurman also took me to meet his mother and other family members.

Meanwhile, Jean and I had become real close friends. People called us twins because we dressed alike, ate lunch together, and sat next to each other in class so we could gossip about what was happening in our lives. I was blindsided by the D I got in history. It was hard to live with, but I overcame it. Jean also got a D. We laughed about it, but it really wasn't funny. I did go on to the eleventh grade the next school year.

Young and Married

Mother finally found her a house and moved out. Thurman and I helped her. I didn't want to transfer to another high school, so she agreed to allow me to stay with Daddy.

One evening when Thurman was at the house (Josie was home too), he said, "Katherine (he did not call me Sissy when he was upset), you're doing a lot of hanging out with that boy, you be done got your belly full and—"

Josie cut in, "She already got her belly full."

I said, "What are you talking about? You don't know what you're talking about."

Josie said, "Girl, I've been watching you; I know you are pregnant."

Daddy said, "Who gonna take care of you?"

Thurman spoke up and said, "I will, Mr. Joe, I'll take care of her."

I don't know what Josie had been watching because I had not missed a period. *She just wants me to get in trouble*, I thought.

Josie took me to the clinic to get a pregnancy test. I was three months pregnant! I was not showing at first, but about two weeks later, my stomach grew to the size of a foot tub. That meant, I could not go back to school; I could not reach my goal. I was so disappointed in myself. My mind flashed back on a phrase I heard my aunt Lena said to someone: "You've made your bed, now lie in it because you can't lie in mine." So true!

Thurman told Daddy and me that we would get married. I told them we would get married just to give the baby a last name, and when it was born we would get a divorce because I wanted to complete school. Thurman later told me he just agreed to that arrangement to appease me, but he never intended on getting a divorce. We got married November 17, 1967. We were both seventeen.

It was Daddy's birthday also. Two weeks later, Daddy had a stroke. Therapy was helping and, with prayers, we all thought he was going to get better. We could only understand some of the words he spoke. I told Daddy that I was going to finish school. He smiled, nodded his head somewhat, and tried to say something. I couldn't understand what he was trying to say, and it was frustrating him so I stopped him from trying to speak.

After the birth of our first son (February 1, 1968), we held him up in front of Daddy to see. He gave me a smile and reached for him. We put him in his hands but held on. I had never seen him helpless before. I never expected this. Daddies are supposed to be there forever, I felt. Soon after that he had another stroke, and it left his right side completely paralyzed. Daddy saw our second son on December 24, 1968, the same way he saw our firstborn. Daddy passed away the following year on December 17, 1969.

Thurman took care of us as he had promised Daddy, but our marriage later failed and, after three sons, it ended in a divorce. I believe it was mainly due to our lack of maturity, communication, and trust. Marriage is good and was instituted by God, but I don't think children should be allowed to marry. Because we were only seventeen, we had to have a cosigner on our marriage license! I considered it a blessing to have had someone who wanted to try to make a wrong (pregnancy out of wedlock) right, by getting married. I can truly say that God never meant for me to marry at such a young age. This came about because of sin, but God forgives.

Starting All Over

At twenty-three, I had the pleasure of meeting my biological father for the first time. I believe he knew where I was all the time; he was just waiting for the perfect moment to be introduced. Uncle James, one of my mother's brothers, introduced him. I did not know what to call him, so I didn't address him by name. When I wasn't around him I called him Pops. After I had known him about four years, I started calling him Dad. He had a special get-together at his home to introduce my family. That is when his brother, the principal I spoke of earlier, told me he knew about me the day he made that visit to see Daddy to discuss why my brother and I were not in school.

I was attending college in Huntsville, Alabama, when my biological father called me, asking if I would come and care for him. He was sick and did not want to go to a nursing facility. My six-year-old son and I moved back to Tennessee to honor his request. (My other two sons were grown and living on their own.) I spent sixteen years with him before he passed away on February 8, 1989 in his home, just as he had desired. I did not return to Huntsville. Dad was generous in giving, but I still wondered who spent the money Grandpa left for me.

My mother assisted me with my six-year-old while I completed my bachelor's degree. It was a joy to have her around. We sat around and talked about life, her upbringing, and her Cherokee mother. I was the last child Mother saw before closing her eyes on December 22, 1998. I pray I will be the first she sees in heaven.

I have had hardships, struggles, trials, and tears, but how immeasurably richer and more satisfying my life is as a result of following God's will. I must remember to follow the example of Jesus when I feel that I deserve better treatment than what I have received—thinking about his sacrifice on the cross. I admit some circumstances in my life have not been as easy to overcome as others, even with the Lord in my life. But with patience and time I got through them. The scars will forever remain. A tear might flow sometimes when I reflect back, but this I know:

> The battle is not mine, but God's
> Because I am not wrestling against flesh and blood, but against principalities,
> Against powers, against the rulers of the darkness of this world,
> Against spiritual wickedness in high places (Ephesians 6:12), that only God can win.

I must allow Him to take over. I thank Him for giving me life and sparing it so many times. "God, thank You for allowing me the opportunity to forgive those who trespassed against me, even the ones who are now deceased." I realize I will never stop forgiving because evil will not stop. It will only intensify the closer I get to God, so as to destroy my faith.

God has built deep within me a compassion for the downtrodden that surpasses the understanding of man. I often find myself in defense of others while I am the one being persecuted (I should have been a defense attorney). God's grace is sufficient for all. His mission is for all, and His gifts are individual. Everything God has planned for me to do will not be easy. I'm sure some things will make my knees tremble, but it must be carried out—for this I live.

"O Lord, our God, you are worthy to receive all glory, honor and power because you are the one who created all things. By your own choice you created them and by your power they continue to exist" (Revelation 4:11, CW). **It is For This I Live . . . to be a servant of the Living God**. I don't have the sense it takes to give up.

No one can explain the mystery of life, and although we can choose whom we worship, there is only true life with God. I will have faith in God to see me through any trial. By His grace, I won't crumble. It is for me to be a witness for God while I live.

Naked

God brought me here with nothing on my back,
depending on me to give Him no slack.
He wanted me to follow His steps,
but sometimes I took the lead.
Sometimes His ways seemed hard to bear,
and I'd cry out saying, "This is not fair."
He came to me on several occasions
and said, "This is not the end,
you shall rise up, my friend."
I'd sing His song and I tried to be strong,
but then again something would go wrong.
He said, "You know the trouble with you, I find,
you haven't left ALL your worries behind."
So, I immediately started to pray,
"Lord, take it ALL away."
So, I'm starting over
naked as before
this time in the mind, soul, and heart
never to depart.[7]

---

[7] Katherine Ross, "Naked," original poem, 2014.

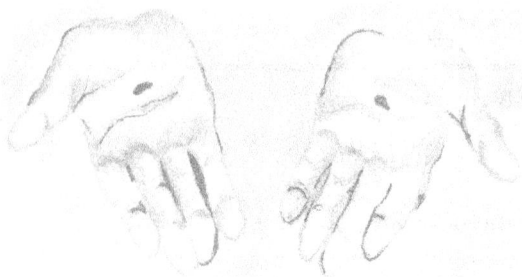

Biography

Born as Katherine Branch on July 20, 1950, she was known as "Sissy" (which she detested), Kat, Lil Kat, or Kathy by family and friends.

Katherine grew up mainly around the rural area of Memphis, Tennessee, on a vegetable farm, except while she was in junior high when she lived in Lakeland, Florida, with her uncle and aunt. She received her GED from Bolton High School while being married, attending night school, and caring for two small sons. Katherine moved to Huntsville, Alabama, in 1986 with her then four-year-old son seeking a degree in religion at Oakwood College. She returned home due to the illness of her biological father.

Katherine completed her BS degree in Biblical Studies at Crichton College in 1992. She worked part time for several years until she secured a full-time job with the Tennessee Board of Probation and Parole.

Katherine professed her commitment to God at the age of nine, and if you were to ask her today who raised her, she would say, "God raised me. My life is all about what I can do for Him. He did not call me because of intellectual greatness—I have none. He called me because I am an empty and willing vessel, seeking constantly to be guided by Him Who created me and gave me breath of life." She has been instrumental in leading numerous friends, family members, and others to Jesus.

She admits to being tripped up by situations in life but never giving up. She realizes that there is an ever-present spiritual battle going on, and there is nothing that can separate her from the love of God (Romans 8:35).

Katherine was the first female elder in Breath of Life Church. She was ordained January 25, 1992. Katherine has three sons: Joseph, Tavis, and Kendrick.